Did You Know?
CARDIFF
A MISCELLANY

Compiled by Julia Skinner
With particular reference to the work of John Milnes

THE FRANCIS FRITH COLLECTION

First published in the United Kingdom in 2006 by The Francis Frith Collection®

This edition published exclusively for Oakridge in 2010 ISBN 978-1-84589-527-3

Did You Know? Cardiff - A Miscellany
Compiled by Julia Skinner
With particular reference to the work of John Milnes

The Francis Frith Collection
Frith's Barn, Teffont,
Salisbury, Wiltshire SP3 5QP
Tel: +44 (0) 1722 716 376
Email: info@francisfrith.co.uk
www.francisfrith.com

Printed and bound in Malaysia

Front Cover: **CARDIFF, CHURCH STREET 1925** 77429p

The colour-tinting is for illustrative purposes only, and is not intended to be historically accurate

CONTENTS

INTRODUCTION

The lively modern city of Cardiff, capital of Wales, stands on historic foundations. The Romans established a fort here, and later the first Norman castle was built about 1091 by Robert Fitzhamon, Lord of Gloucester, as a motte and bailey fortification. Cardiff began to establish itself as an important trading centre and port in Elizabethan times, but was also known to be a den of cut-throats and pirates, many of whom were drawn to the town from their base on the island of Flat Holm in the Bristol Channel.

During the Civil War, the Lord of Cardiff, the 5th Earl of Pembroke, was a Parliamentary sympathiser, but most of the gentry of Glamorgan were Royalist. Cardiff Castle was taken and occupied by a Royalist garrison. However, by the time of the Royalist defeat at the battle of Naseby in 1645, the Welsh were no longer willing to support the king's cause. Charles I sought refuge at Cardiff Castle, but help was refused him and most of South Wales passed into the hands of Parliament. The king observed: 'The hearts of the people of Wales are as hard and rocky as their country.'

By the 1780s the town was in decline, with a population of about 1,500 people. However, the Industrial Revolution was to turn Cardiff into 'Coalopolis', one of the busiest ports in the country, exporting Welsh coal to all over the world.

In 1794 the area was transformed by the opening of the Glamorgan Canal, linking the ironworks, and later the coalfields, around Merthyr Tydfil with the port of Cardiff. The local landowner, the 2nd Marquess of Bute, realised that with industrialisation the demand for coal was growing, and saw the opportunity to exploit this by developing the port. This far-sighted idea was the making of Cardiff. The Marquess saw that a deep-water dock would be needed to cater for the larger ships which were being developed,

and the West Bute dock was opened in 1839. The volume of traffic very soon meant that a second dock was needed, and the East Bute dock opened in 1855. At its peak in 1913, the port of Cardiff exported 13 million tons of coal.

But this was not to last. After the end of the First World War, Winston Churchill restored the Gold Standard, making Welsh coal expensive. The coal industry declined throughout the United Kingdom during the 20th century, and the fortunes of Cardiff declined with it. Ironically, in the 21st century the coal being handled by the South Wales docks is more likely to be imported, low-grade Polish coal for power stations than exported Welsh coal. However, the city's 19th-century civic buildings are the jewel in Cardiff's crown, and Cardiff Castle, turned into a medieval fantasy by the 3rd Marquess of Bute, remains a monument to the wealth that was created by the Welsh coal miners.

But Cardiff is not a backward-looking city, despite its proud and important place in history; in the 21st century Cardiff is reinventing itself in spectacular fashion. Tourism and the leisure industry have become important to the city's economy; the former tidal basin is now a fresh-water lake and a water-bus allows exploration of its eight-mile waterfront. The city landscape is filling with stunning modern developments, and its Millennium Stadium will be seen by television viewers the world over when London hosts the 2012 Olympic Games, as the Stadium will be the venue for at least 8 of the football events.

The story of Cardiff is full of colourful characters, events and stories, of which this book can only provide a brief glimpse.

WELSH WORDS AND PHRASES

In early times the name of Cardiff was spelt in various ways, often with a K - 'Kerdiff' for instance - and in fact, that is how many Cardiffians pronounce the name today.

Not much Welsh is spoken nowadays in Cardiff, but if you want to be adventurous, here are a few phrases:

'Thankyou' is ***'Diolch'.***

'Good Health' or 'Cheers' is ***'Iechydd Da'.***

'Hello' is ***'Shw mae'.***

'Goodbye' is ***'Hwyl'.***

'Good morning' is ***'Bore da'.***

'Good day' is ***'Dydd da'.***

HAUNTED CARDIFF

The National Museum of Wales in Cardiff is believed to be haunted by the ghost of Dunbar Smith, the architect of the building, who was offended when his ashes were removed to make way for a public toilet.

Cardiff Castle is the subject of several ghostly tales. The spectre of the 2nd Marquess of Bute, who began the restoration of the castle, is said to sometimes appear, walking through the library fireplace; he then passes through a thick stone wall into a corridor, then through the wall of the chapel, finally ending his journey in the room in which he died in 1848. Another blurred, ghostly shape has also been seen in a stockroom of the castle, where items get mysteriously disarranged, and the dining hall also suffers unexplained manifestations, with lights flashing on and off, and heavy doors apparently being opened and shut by an invisible hand.

The woods around Castell Coch, near Cardiff, are said to be haunted by Dame Griffiths, who died of grief after her young son drowned in a pool.

Caerphilly Castle eight miles north of Cardiff is haunted by the shade of a 'green lady', who moves from turret to turret, as well as by ghostly soldiers. Some staff have reported smelling a strong scent of perfume in the flag tower for no obvious reason.

CARDIFF MISCELLANY

Cardiff's City Hall was completed in 1904; the architect was E A Rickards, a devotee of the baroque style. The dome over the entrance pavilion is topped by an impressive lead dragon.

One of the outstanding features of the interior of the City Hall is the Marble Hall, on the first floor, with its monolithic columns of Siena marble. It houses eleven specially commissioned statues of Welsh and Celtic figures, of which the central figure is Dewi Sant, or St David. In the Lord Mayor's parlour is a priceless mosaic picture made from 86,000 pieces of Italian marble. This was a present from the King of Italy to Sir Thomas Morel, the Mayor of Cardiff.

Simple yet unusual and striking, The Welsh National War Memorial is situated in the Alexandra Gardens part of Cathays Park (see pages 34-35). It is a double circular colonnade enclosing the Cenotaph. It was designed by J Ninian Cooper and unveiled in June 1928 by the Prince of Wales.

Victoria Park used to house a small zoo where Billy the Seal was a firm favourite. He is now commemorated with a sculpture which stands in the park.

Before the town council renamed it, Queen Street was called Crockherbtown, allegedly because the monks of Greyfriars used to grow pots of herbs there.

The two groups of statuary flanking the large ornate window of the Council Chamber (photograph 77441, below) represent the sea receiving the three rivers of the city - the Taff, the Rhymney and the Ely. Groups of sculpture representing music and poetry and Welsh unity and patriotism surmount the pavilions. Other sculpted figures on the clock tower represent the four winds.

CITY HALL 1925 77441

THE DOCKS 1893 32696

Shallow-draught paddle-steamers were developed specifically for use in the tidal estuaries, where the water level could be very low. The steamer in the foreground of photograph 32696, above, is the 'Success', a working boat.

Lavernock Point, near Penarth, is an important site in the history of communications. It was from here in 1897 that Marconi sent the first radio transmission over water to the islet of Flat Holm. A blue plaque set into the boundary wall of nearby Lavernock Church records the event.

Just outside Cardiff, at St Fagans, is the award-winning Museum of Welsh Life. Here, more than 30 original Welsh buildings and cottages have been constructed to give visitors a flavour of Welsh life in the past.

The stepping stones seen in photograph 56486, below, are no ordinary stepping stones, for they are perfectly circular and their line - across the River Ely - is perfectly accurate. The 3rd Earl of Plymouth had inherited the castle and lands, and in 1870 he employed the distinguished landscape gardener, James Pulham, to create some grandiose gardens. His final task was to construct this river crossing, known as the Ogmore Stones.

ST FAGANS, THE STEPPING STONES 1906 56486

CARDIFF ARMS PARK c1960 C23182

LLANDOUGH, ST DOCHDWY'S CHURCH c1955 L280012

Llandough was the site of a Celtic monastery founded by St Dochdwy or Dochau, the name by which St Cyngar was better known. The present church is of the 19th century (see photograph L280012, above), but in the churchyard is a highly-decorated cross of the early 9th century. Although ravaged by the weather, the cross has an interlaced pattern of ropework, below which are various sculptures, including a horse-rider.

It is perhaps difficult today to appreciate the commercial standing of Cardiff in the early 20th century. Just prior to the First World War nearly 50 nations had representatives based in the area.

Roath Park was laid out in 1894 at a cost of £62,000 - a considerable sum in those days. The land was presented to the city by the Bute estate. The lake extended to 32 acres, and once incorporated a swimming pool. Lady Sophia, the wife of the 2nd Marquess of Bute, played a large part in creating what has been described as a 'mini-Kew' garden.

It is quite possible that the attendant pictured in the boat in photograph 49001 (below) is the much-loved 'Sammy the Boatman'. Described as 'the friend of the children' in his obituary in The Western Mail, the Norwegian-born Mr Stephenson superintended bathing in the lake for 31 years. It was said that the sound of his whistle would cause birds to flock to eat out of his hand.

ROATH PARK LAKE 1902 49001

Greyfriars House was built for William Herbert c1570, utilising the old Franciscan friary on the site as a quarry, the friary having been closed at the Dissolution. The mansion fell into ruin itself by the late 18th century. The endeavours of the 3rd and 4th Marquesses of Bute saw the site excavated, footings laid out and eventually fenced in as public space. Thus protected from the construction of Greyfriars Road, Cardiffians believed that the site and its ruin were forever preserved (see photograph below).

The highly controversial sale of the site around 1960 resulted in the demolition of the ruins and the construction of the towering Pearl Assurance building in 1967. Now named the Capital Tower, the passing years have diminished the shock of its size and scale, with its dominance of the city skyline challenged by more recent building projects.

THE FRIARY RUINS, (GREYFRIARS HOUSE), CATHAYS PARK c1955 C23077

THE CAPITAL TOWER
(THE SITE OF THE OLD FRIARY RUINS) 2004 C23735

THE INTERNATIONAL ARENA 2004 C23719

Opened by Queen Elizabeth II in 1993, the Cardiff International
Centre is described by its owners as the 'complete venue'
(see photograph C23719, above). Its facilities are certainly
impressive. Apart from its role as a 5,500-seat concert venue
the vast events complex was also designed to house a wide
selection of corporate and conference suites and the globally-
linked Cardiff World Trade Centre.

In the Welsh Folk Museum at St Fagan's is an ornate triple harp
which was made for the Great Exhibition of 1851 by the royal harp-
maker Bassett Jones, of Cardiff. A triple harp has strings arranged
in three rows, and became known as 'the Welsh harp' because of its
popularity with Welsh harpists.

It was said in the 19th century that South Wales coal ran the British Navy - much of it would have passed through Cardiff.

The rich terracotta brick Pier Head building seen to the right of photograph 77413 (below) was constructed in 1886 as offices for the Bute Dock Company. In 1922 the building was taken over by the Great Western Railway, whose acquisition of every South Wales port instantly made them the world's largest dock owner.

THE GREAT WESTERN OFFICES 1925 77413

SOPHIA GARDENS 1896 38711

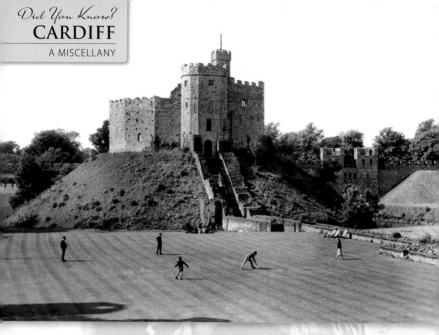

CARDIFF CASTLE, THE OLD KEEP c1960 C23140

The ruined stone Norman keep stands on the motte (or mound) of the earliest castle that was built soon after the Norman Conquest, and is exceptionally well preserved (see photograph C23140, above). Ringed by its own moat, and steeply stepped, it sat within the castle grounds serving as a second line of defence from marauders and invaders.

Cardiff University was founded in 1833. The main University building is located in Cathays Park. The Applied Science departments are situated on the original site of the college in Newport Road.

One of Cardiff's most famous sons was Ivor Novello, actor, composer and playwright, who was born in Canton, Cardiff in 1893.

Sophia Gardens can be regarded as the city's first public park. In 1857 the widow of the 2nd Marquess resolved to 'set a noble example to other towns' and presented the people of Cardiff with a pleasure ground of 'exquisite taste and design'. The Pavilion, shown below, which used to stand in Sophia Gardens was built in 1951, originally part of Cardiff's contribution to the Festival of Britain; the inaugural concert starred Danny Kaye. A heavy snowfall in January 1982 caused its roof to collapse, leading to the eventual demolition of the building.

SOPHIA GARDENS, THE PAVILION c1960 C23171

LLANDAFF, THE CATHEDRAL 1893 32699

The ancient city of Llandaff, whose name means 'the sacred enclosure on the River Taff', is just two miles north of Cardiff. The cathedral is one of the earliest ecclesiastical foundations in Britain, founded by St Dyfrig in the 6th century (see photograph 32699, above). In the 19th century the cathedral was much restored, but was badly damaged by a German landmine in 1941; among British cathedrals, only Coventry suffered more damage.

Following the war damage to Llandaff Cathedral the interior was repaired in bold style: an arch now spans the nave, carrying Sir Jacob Epstein's aluminium figure of Christ in Majesty (seen in photograph C23777, opposite).

HIGH STREET 2004 C23727

The Goat Major public house in High Street was formerly called the Blue Bell (see photograph C23727, above). The recent change of name is in tribute to strong Welsh regimental links to Cardiff.

It was the 2nd Marquess of Bute who foresaw the need to turn Cardiff into a deep-water port. The West Bute dock was opened in 1839 at a cost of £350,000. This was considered to be 'the largest venture undertaken by anyone anywhere in the world at his own expense'. The volume of traffic was so great that another dock, the East Bute dock, which was built parallel to its precursor, was opened in 1855.

Cardiff's Millennium Stadium, with its distinctive skyline masts, is now well-known nationally, thanks to its role hosting the FA Cup final - a match screened nationwide. Built for the 1999 Rugby World Cup, it has a capacity almost 50% greater than the old National Stadium.

To demonstrate its belief in the viability of a redeveloped waterfront the County Council relocated its headquarters there in 1988. Thus the £28-million 'Giant Pagoda' became the first significant building of the new Cardiff Bay (see photograph C23779, below).

COUNTY HALL 2004 C23779

CARDIFF CASTLE 1893 32667

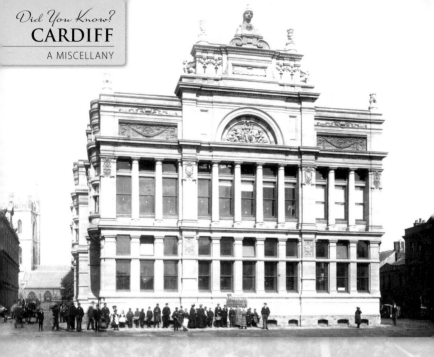

THE LIBRARY 1896 38710

A bust of Minerva sits proudly atop the grand Hayes façade of the library extension, which was opened in 1896 (see photograph 38710, above).

A major attraction at Cardiff Bay is Techniquest, a museum with a difference. There are around 160 exhibits at this 'hands on' science and technology discovery centre. It encourages visitors, and particularly school children, to become actively involved in understanding scientific principles in an entertaining way.

The 3rd Marquess of Bute was a skilled linguist who mastered 21 different languages.

The carving in Llandaff Cathedral known as the three faces and four eyes represents the three Celtic saints of the present cathedral - St Dyfrig (the founder), his successor St Teilo, and Teilo's nephew Euddogwy (see photograph L67046, below).

LLANDAFF, THE CATHEDRAL, A CAPITAL - THREE FACES AND FOUR EYES c1955 L67046

Many academics scoff at Cardiff Castle, claiming that with its diversity of styles and influences it is not a true castle - however it is indeed an authentic castle. What makes it unique is that it is the combined work of many building periods, from Roman right up to Victorian renovations. The Romans erected a wooden fort on this site in the 1st century, and the Normans replaced it with a medieval stronghold: the castle has a 1,900-year-old history of repelling invaders. In the medieval period a moat was a necessity, but in later years it was filled in. When the famous landscape gardener 'Capability' Brown was commissioned by the 1st Marquess of Bute to landscape the grounds in the 1760s, he reopened the moat, in the form of an ornamental lake.

The town of Caerphilly, eight miles north of Cardiff, is the home of Caerphilly Castle, one of Europe's finest medieval military monuments. Along with Windsor and Dover, this vast fortress is one of the largest castles in Britain, and covers over 30 acres. Dating from the 13th century, it is not just a monument in stone; the water defences are equally impressive. Caerphilly Castle has a tipsy leaning tower, probably caused by an attempt to blow it up during the Civil War; the degree from the perpendicular is greater than that of the Leaning Tower of Pisa.

At the southern end of the lake in Roath Park is a clock tower built in the form of a lighthouse (photograph C23761, right). This commemorates Captain Scott's ill-fated expedition to the South Pole; his ship, the 'Terra Nova', sailed from Cardiff in 1910.

The wealth of the Bute family, creators of the Cardiff docklands, was displayed loud and clear at their castle home. The 3rd Marquess of Bute, reputedly the richest man in the world in his day, commissioned the opium-smoking genius William Burges to transform his residence into a no-expense-spared medieval fantasy palace decorated with astonishing detail. This folly of all follies can still be seen in all its glory, for medieval banquets now take place here.

ROATH PARK 2004 C23761

ST MARY STREET 1896 38709

Photograph 38709, above, shows the statue of the 2nd Marquess of Bute (seen from the rear), quite literally 'master of all he surveys', in its earlier position in St Mary Street. However he had to give way to modern traffic requirements, and since 2000 the statue has been at Bute Square.

S A Brain & Co have brewed beer in Cardiff for over a century. One of their famous slogans was 'It's Brains you want', and the nickname for their popular Brains S A is 'Skull Attack'.

The National Museum of Wales in Cardiff boasts an outstanding collection of French Impressionist paintings, with works by Cezanne, Monet, Renoir and Van Gogh.

Cardiff has a perfect Edwardian Civic Centre, precise in scale and scope. It was built in Portland stone around 1904, and most of the buildings put up since have been designed with an empathy for the whole (see photograph 54941, below).

THE CITY HALL AND THE LAW COURTS 1906 54941

THE WAR MEMORIAL c1950 C23058

BUTE DOCKS 1925 77418

Since the halcyon days of 1913 the docks' export tonnage was in steady decline, recovering briefly during the fuel demands of the First World War. 1925 was to prove a fateful year for the port. Churchill's decision to return Britain to the Gold Standard of 1914 instantly made Welsh coal much more expensive than that of its competitors, effectively pricing it out of the market, and reducing the shipping that would use the docks.

Cardiff was granted city status by Edward VII in 1905.

The historic site of St Fagans Castle lies four miles west of Cardiff. The castle was originally of the 13th century, but is now more of a gabled mansion. In 1648 it was the scene of one of the bloodiest battles in the Civil War, when Parliamentarian soldiers in South Wales staged a rebellion because they had not been paid; they were defeated by a loyal Parliamentarian force under the command of Colonel Thomas Horton.

Cardiff's port kept ahead of technology - massive cranes on tracks were developed, which could lift an entire coal wagon and dump it into the ship's hold, but by the time of photograph C23102 (below) the 'coal rush' of Cardiff was in decline.

THE DOCKS c1955 C23102

CARDIFF CASTLE 1893 32672

A will in verse written by Owen Powell of Cardiff in 1897 made his
bequest very clear:

When my Wife's a Widow of me bereft,
She shall inherit all I've left;
And when she's finished her career,
It shall then go to my Daughters dear.
In equal shares to save all bother,
Not flesh to one and fish the other,
They are all kind and dear to me,
So no distinction shall there be.

Cardiff Arms Park is the Taff-side home of the famous 'Blue & Blacks'. The club was formed in 1876, and the ground took its name from the nearby Cardiff Arms Hotel, which was demolished in 1878. Such was the fame of the club ground that to rugby fans the world over its name and that of the National Stadium were virtually synonymous. In the summer Glamorgan's cricketers played on its well-manicured turf until 1966; they moved to a new ground at Sophia Gardens in 1967.

The Norwegian Church Arts Centre, overlooking Cardiff Bay, was originally a place of worship for sailors from the Norwegian Merchant Navy fleet; up to 75,000 sailors a year would visit this church in the 19th century. It fell into disrepair in the 20th century, but in 1987 a trust fund was set up for its restoration, under the guidance of the author Roald Dahl, whose parents were Norwegian and who was christened in the church after being born in Cardiff in 1916. It reopened in its new role as an arts centre in 1992.

ROATH PARK 1896 38714

CITY HALL 1925 77433

The first Norman castle is thought to have been built in Cardiff c1091, on the site of a previous Welsh fortification. Extra defensive height was achieved by piling the spoil on the top of the circuit walls to create a rampart. In 1106 Robert Curthose, Duke of Normandy, waged an unsuccessful war with Henry I; the defeated duke was taken to Cardiff Castle. Curthose's eyes were put out, and he remained a prisoner until his death in 1134.

Recorded on a grave in Cardiff:

Here rest my Spouse; no pair through life
So equal lived as we did.
Alike we shared perpetual strife,
Nor knew I rest till she did.

SPORTING CARDIFF

Cardiff City's victory in the 1927 FA Cup final, 1-0 against Arsenal, was notable for a number of reasons. Most famously, it was the only occasion on which the cup has been taken out of England. Ironically, the game was played on St George's Day. The win came only seven years after the club entered the football league, and only seventeen after it turned professional. The match also marked a new era in sports reporting, being the first one broadcast live on radio. The 1920s were a glorious time for the club. They were Division One runners-up in 1924, and FA Cup finalists for the first time in 1925.

The Wales National Ice Rink is home to the successful Cardiff Devils ice hockey team.

Cardiff can boast of having produced two of the most famous British athletes of modern times. Dame Tanni Grey-Thompson, OBE, MBE, has won eleven Paralympic gold medals. She has a long list of achievements to her name, including twice being named 'Welsh Sports Personality of the Year', and being the only Paralympian in the World Sports Academy 'Hall of Fame'. Born in Cardiff in 1969, Tanni was named Carys Davina, but was given the nickname 'tiny' by her sister, which stuck and became Tanni. Colin Jackson, also Cardiff born, had an immensely successful career in the 110-metre hurdles, through the late 1980s and 1990s. He won two world championships, in 1993 and 1999, an Olympic silver medal in 1988, and four European championships. Between 1993 and 2006 he held the World Record for the 110 metre hurdles with a time of 12.91 seconds, which was set on 20 August 1993 in Stuttgart, Germany.

Cardiff Rugby Club has produced some fine players, including Wales and British Lions half-backs Gareth Edwards and Barry John, and the three-quarter Gerald Davies.

The Millennium Stadium, and its predecessor, the National Stadium, are and were internationally renowned venues. They have witnessed some notable and unusual events: in 1941 the North Stand of the National Stadium was demolished by a German landmine; in 1988 rugby player Paul Thorburn set a world record for a long range penalty kick - 70 yards 8.5 inches; and in 2001 the first competitive football match under a closed roof was played in the Millennium Stadium between Liverpool and Manchester United in the FA Community Shield.

Did You Know?
CARDIFF
A MISCELLANY

QUIZ QUESTIONS

Answers on page 49.

1. What does the name 'Cardiff' mean?

2. In which year did Cardiff become the capital of Wales?

3. There is a statue of which historical figure in Cardiff's City Hall, and why might some people find this surprising?

4. Which famous singer came from the area of Cardiff popularly known as Tiger Bay?

5. When and where would you have seen real Cowboys and Indians in Cardiff?

6. What is the link between Llandaff and the United States of America?

7. What twinning 'first' did Cardiff achieve?

8. The first British news film ever recorded was of an event in Cardiff in 1896. What was it?

9. Which Cardiff-born footballer became the youngest player ever to be capped for Wales in 1991?

10. In a survey in 1999 on 'the best city in the UK in which to work', in which position did Cardiff come?

CAERPHILLY, THE CASTLE 1896 38733

RECIPE

GLAMORGAN SAUSAGES

Ingredients

150g/5oz fresh breadcrumbs
150g/5oz grated Caerphilly cheese
1 small leek, very finely chopped
1 tablespoon chopped fresh parsley
Leaves from 1 sprig of thyme, chopped
2 eggs
1½ teaspoons English mustard powder
3 tablespoons milk
Plain flour, for coating
1 tablespoon oil
1 tablespoon melted butter
Salt and pepper

Mix the breadcrumbs, cheese, leek, herbs and seasoning. Whisk the eggs with the mustard and reserve 2 tablespoons of the mixture. Stir the rest into the cheese mixture with enough milk to bind. Divide the cheese mixture into eight and form into sausage shapes. Dip the sausage in the reserved egg to coat. Season the flour, then roll the sausages in it to give a light, even coating. Chill for about 30 minutes until firm. Preheat the grill and oil the grill rack. Mix the oil and melted butter together and brush over the sausages. Grill the sausages for about 5-10 minutes, turning carefully, until golden brown all over. Serve hot or cold.

THE HAYES LOOKING TOWARDS WORKING STREET 1925 77426

QUEEN STREET 1893 32678

RECIPE

BARA BRITH - SPECKLED BREAD

Ingredients
1 mug strong cold tea
4 tablespoons marmalade
175g/6oz sultanas
250g/8oz soft brown sugar
425g/12oz self-raising flour
2 beaten eggs
A good pinch of mixed spice.

Soak the fruit and marmalade in the cold tea for at least one hour, although overnight is best. Then add the sugar, flour, beaten eggs and spice. Mix together well and put into a greased loaf tin. Bake for about 1½ hours at 150 degrees C/300 degees F/Gas Mark 5. Delicious served in slices spread with butter.

CHURCH STREET 1925 77429

QUIZ ANSWERS

1. There are two possible interpretations of the name Cardiff. The first is that Cardiff derives its name from the Welsh 'caer', meaning 'fort', and 'dyf', a form of the name for the River Taff that flows through the city. The second interpretation is that the city takes its name from the Roman general Aulus Didius: 'Caer Didi', meaning 'fort of Didius'.

2. Cardiff became the capital of Wales in 1955, making it one of Europe's youngest capital cities.

3. There is a statue of the Welsh freedom fighter Owain Glyndwr in Cardiff's City Hall, despite the fact that he razed Cardiff to the ground in 1404.

4. The waterfront area known as Butetown - better known as Tiger Bay - was the birthplace in 1937 of the singer Shirley Bassey.

5. In September 1891, when Buffalo Bill's Wild West Show was staged in Sophia Gardens.

6. A famous son of Llandaff, just outside Cardiff, was Francis Lewis, who was born there in 1713; he was one of the signatories of the American Declaration of Independence.

7. Cardiff was the first UK city to twin with a city in China (Xiamen).

8. The visit of the Prince and Princess of Wales to the Cardiff Exhibition.

9. Ryan Giggs, who was capped for Wales at the age of 17 years, 321 days.

10. Top!

THE MILLENNIUM STADIUM
2004 C23713

CHEMISTS
BOOKSELLERS
AND
STATIONERS

FRANCIS FRITH

PIONEER VICTORIAN PHOTOGRAPHER

Francis Frith, founder of the world-famous photographic archive, was a complex and multi-talented man. A devout Quaker and a highly successful Victorian businessman, he was philosophical by nature and pioneering in outlook. By 1855 he had already established a wholesale grocery business in Liverpool, and sold it for the astonishing sum of £200,000, which is the equivalent today of over £15,000,000. Now in his thirties, and captivated by the new science of photography, Frith set out on a series of pioneering journeys up the Nile and to the Near East.

INTRIGUE AND EXPLORATION

He was the first photographer to venture beyond the sixth cataract of the Nile. Africa was still the mysterious 'Dark Continent', and Stanley and Livingstone's historic meeting was a decade into the future. The conditions for picture taking confound belief. He laboured for hours in his wicker dark-room in the sweltering heat of the desert, while the volatile chemicals fizzed dangerously in their trays. Back in London he exhibited his photographs and was 'rapturously cheered' by members of the Royal Society. His reputation as a photographer was made overnight.

VENTURE OF A LIFE-TIME

By the 1870s the railways had threaded their way across the country, and Bank Holidays and half-day Saturdays had been made obligatory by Act of Parliament. All of a sudden the working man and his family were able to enjoy days out, take holidays, and see a little more of the world.

With typical business acumen, Francis Frith foresaw that these new tourists would enjoy having souvenirs to commemorate their days out. For the next thirty years he travelled the country by train and by pony and trap, producing fine photographs of seaside resorts and beauty spots that were keenly bought by millions of Victorians. These prints were painstakingly pasted into family albums and pored over during the dark nights of winter, rekindling precious memories of summer excursions. Frith's studio was soon supplying retail shops all over the country, and by 1890 F Frith & Co had become the greatest specialist photographic publishing company in the world, with over 2,000 sales outlets, and pioneered the picture postcard.

FRANCIS FRITH'S LEGACY

Francis Frith had died in 1898 at his villa in Cannes, his great project still growing. By 1970 the archive he created contained over a third of a million pictures showing 7,000 British towns and villages.

Frith's legacy to us today is of immense significance and value, for the magnificent archive of evocative photographs he created provides a unique record of change in the cities, towns and villages throughout Britain over a century and more. Frith and his fellow studio photographers revisited locations many times down the years to update their views, compiling for us an enthralling and colourful pageant of British life and character.

We are fortunate that Frith was dedicated to recording the minutiae of everyday life. For it is this sheer wealth of visual data, the painstaking chronicle of changes in dress, transport, street layouts, buildings, housing and landscape that captivates us so much today, offering us a powerful link with the past and with the lives of our ancestors.

Computers have now made it possible for Frith's many thousands of images to be accessed almost instantly. The archive offers every one of us an opportunity to examine the places where we and our families have lived and worked down the years. Its images, depicting our shared past, are now bringing pleasure and enlightenment to millions around the world a century and more after his death.

For further information visit: www.francisfrith.com

INTERIOR DECORATION

Frith's photographs can be seen framed and as giant wall murals in thousands of pubs, restaurants, hotels, banks, retail stores and other public buildings throughout Britain. These provide interesting and attractive décor, generating strong local interest and acting as a powerful reminder of gentler days in our increasingly busy and frenetic world.

FRITH PRODUCTS

All Frith photographs are available as prints and posters in a variety of different sizes and styles. In the UK we also offer a range of other gift and stationery products illustrated with Frith photographs, although many of these are not available for delivery outside the UK – see our web site for more information on the products available for delivery in your country.

THE INTERNET

Over 100,000 photographs of Britain can be viewed and purchased on the Frith web site. The web site also includes memories and reminiscences contributed by our customers, who have personal knowledge of localities and of the people and properties depicted in Frith photographs. If you wish to learn more about a specific town or village you may find these reminiscences fascinating to browse. Why not add your own comments if you think they would be of interest to others? See **www.francisfrith.com**

PLEASE HELP US BRING FRITH'S PHOTOGRAPHS TO LIFE

Our authors do their best to recount the history of the places they write about. They give insights into how particular towns and villages developed, they describe the architecture of streets and buildings, and they discuss the lives of famous people who lived there. But however knowledgeable our authors are, the story they tell is necessarily incomplete.

Frith's photographs are so much more than plain historical documents. They are living proofs of the flow of human life down the generations. They show real people at real moments in history; and each of those people is the son or daughter of someone, the brother or sister, aunt or uncle, grandfather or grandmother of someone else. All of them lived, worked and played in the streets depicted in Frith's photographs.

We would be grateful if you would give us your insights into the places shown in our photographs: the streets and buildings, the shops, businesses and industries. Post your memories of life in those streets on the Frith website: what it was like growing up there, who ran the local shop and what shopping was like years ago; if your workplace is shown tell us about your working day and what the building is used for now. Read other visitors' memories and reconnect with your shared local history and heritage. With your help more and more Frith photographs can be brought to life, and vital memories preserved for posterity, and for the benefit of historians in the future.

Wherever possible, we will try to include some of your comments in future editions of our books. Moreover, if you spot errors in dates, titles or other facts, please let us know, because our archive records are not always completely accurate—they rely on 140 years of human endeavour and hand-compiled records. You can email us using the contact form on the website.

Thank you!

For further information, trade, or author enquiries
please contact us at the address below:

**The Francis Frith Collection, Frith's Barn, Teffont,
Salisbury, Wiltshire, England SP3 5QP.**
Tel: +44 (0)1722 716 376 Fax: +44 (0)1722 716 881
e-mail: sales@francisfrith.co.uk **www.francisfrith.com**

RD 02/11